Cooking With Tofu

by Mary Anna DuSablon

What is tofu? It is a delicious, mild-flavored "cheese" made from soybeans. It was invented in Asia about nine or ten thousand years ago, and the reasons for its lasting popularity will become evident as soon as you try it.

A culinary chameleon, tofu takes on the flavors and seasonings of anything with which it is cooked. You can use tofu as a main ingredient, or keep a cake of tofu on hand to add as a thickener, as a protein extender, or as an ingredient in soups, stews, vegetable or egg dishes, and desserts. I like to nibble on it fresh — sometimes with a little soy sauce sprinkled over it.

Tofu looks like ricotta cheese pressed into a dense, congealed square. It has a somewhat chewier consistency than ricotta.

Why eat tofu? Tofu is a low-calorie, low-sodium, cholesterol-free, protein-rich, inexpensive food. It is easily digested. Those who are allergic to lactose in milk can substitute tofu in recipes calling for cream, cream cheese, ricotta, or cottage cheese. It is sometimes used as an egg substitute, as you will see in our mayonnaise recipe. So whether you are concerned about your health, your pocketbook, or both, you will find tofu to be one of the best protein foods you can buy.

COMPOSITION OF FOODS*

100 GRAM PORTIONS	PROTEIN (GRAM)	FAT (GRAM)	CARBO-HYDRATES (GRAM)	CALCIUM (MG)	IRON (MG)
Tofu	7.8	4.2	2.4	128	1.9
Ground beef (cooked)	24	20	—	11	3.2
Eggs	13	11.5	0.9	54	2.3
Cream cheese	8.2	37.6	2.4	62	0.2
Sour cream	3	20.4	4.3	102	.04
Cow's milk	3.5	3.7	4.9	117	—
Yogurt	3	3.4	4.9	111	—

100 GRAM PORTIONS	SODIUM (MG)	POTASSIUM (MG)	VIT. A (I.U.)	VIT. B_1 (MG)	VIT. B_2 (MG)	VIT. B_3 (MG)
Tofu	7	42	—	0.06	0.03	0.1
Ground beef (cooked)	47	450	40	0.09	0.21	5.4
Eggs	122	129	1,180	0.11	0.30	0.1
Cream cheese	250	74	1,541	0.02	0.20	0.1
Sour cream	41	118	839	0.03	0.15	0.04
Cow's milk	50	140	150	0.03	0.17	0.1
Yogurt	47	132	140	0.03	0.16	—

* *Nutritive Value of Foods,* Home and Garden Bulletin #72, USDA: Washington D.C. (1970).

Nutritive Value of American Foods: In Common Units, prepared by Catherine F. Adams, USDA: Washington D. C. (1975).

The No-Nonsense Guide to Food and Nutrition, Marion McGill and Orrea Pye, Butterick Publishing Company: New York (1978).

Made from soybean "milk," tofu is high in usable protein and contains all of the 8 essential amino acids. By eating grains, seeds, nuts, dairy, or meat with your tofu meal, you can boost the amount of this available protein by as much as 40 percent.

Tofu has the lowest fat count of any source of protein, and very little of that is saturated fat. This is particularly important since tofu can be substituted for part or all of the cream, sour cream, or cheese in your cooking, after a little experimentation.

Tofu contains many important vitamins and minerals, the most abundant being calcium. It is also a good source of iron, phosphorus, potassium, the essential B vitamins, choline, and vitamin E.

Enjoying Tofu For the First Time

If you have not enjoyed the taste of tofu yet, you are in for a treat. Start by buying a cake of tofu at the supermarket and trying it in simple recipes. The recipe for Eastern-Western Eggs at the end of this section is an easy recipe to try first.

You can find tofu in most supermarkets in the dairy case or among the oriental vegetables in the produce department. It may be labeled tofu, bean curd, bean cake, or soybean curd; but it is all the same product. It often comes in a plastic container with a see-through plastic top. Inside the 12-ounce or 1-pound package will be a square of tofu covered with water.

If your supermarket does not carry tofu, look for it at a health food store or an oriental food market. A word of advice: tofu does come in cans. I bought some, and it looked unappetizing, felt like rubber, and tasted terrible. If you are trying tofu for the first time, be sure you buy *fresh* tofu.

Keep tofu in the refrigerator. It will last in the refrigerator for about a week, but it will stay fresh longer if you change the water every other day. Once you have opened the tofu package to change the water, transfer the tofu to a container with a lid. I usually store my tofu in a square, plastic, freezer container with a snap-on lid. You can also store tofu in the freezer — for up to 3 months.

If you are in doubt about cooking with tofu — how the texture is to work with, what it tastes like — here is a delicious and foolproof recipe to start with.

EASTERN-WESTERN EGGS

2 tablespoons butter
6 ounces tofu
1/4 cup chopped green onion *or* **cooking onion**
1/4 cup chopped green pepper *or* **mushrooms**
2 to 3 eggs
salt and pepper
3 tablespoons grated cheddar cheese (optional)

Melt the butter in a skillet; then add the tofu, crumbling it up with your hands. Sauté the tofu for 3 minutes, stirring and breaking up the clumps until the tofu is slightly dry. Add the vegetables and continue sautéing another 3 to 4 minutes. Beat the eggs slightly and add them to the mixture. Scramble them until firm, then season to taste. Serve Eastern-Western Eggs with grated cheese on top.

Yield: 2 servings
Time: approximately 10 minutes

Tips for Cooking And Storing Tofu

The water content in *all* tofu differs occasionally, whether store-bought or homemade. You may have to adjust the liquids in your recipes accordingly. Remember, it is easier to add more liquids to a recipe than more dry ingredients.

• To make a firmer or drier tofu, place the tofu on your drainboard, wrapping it with cheesecloth or paper towels. Place a saucer or small dish on top of the tofu and a 1-pound can on top of the dish to press the water out of the tofu. Drain for at least 15 minutes. Parboiling the tofu will also result in a drier product.

• If you wrap tofu in a clean towel and twist and wring the water out, you will have a crumbly, dry tofu — good in stir-fry dishes.

• To use tofu as a thickener for sauces and gravies, make your sauce or gravy thinner than usual. Then whip the tofu in, using a wire whisk. The texture will not be smooth, but it is an interesting consistency, and your sauce will be richer in protein.

• Plan to use fresh, sweet tofu in desserts, salads, and drinks. Cook with tofu that is older or slightly bitter.

• Tofu will last in the refrigerator about 1 week. It will stay fresher if you change the water every other day.

Soybeans are easy to grow. They prefer a sandy loam, well fertilized with lime, potash, and phosphoric acid; but the plant is not too fussy. Sow seeds in early spring, and harvest for dried beans when the plant is brown and bare of leaves, and only the dried pods remain.

• Refrigerated tofu will begin to turn pink around the edges when it is about to go bad. It can be revitalized by parboiling, but should be used soon. To parboil, place the tofu, whole or in slices, in a saucepan; then cover with water. Bring to a boil, then reduce the heat and simmer for about 3 minutes. Remove the tofu with a slotted spoon.

• When your tofu smells yeasty or sour, it should be thrown out.

Frozen Tofu

Tofu can be stored in the freezer for up to 3 months. During the freezing process the tofu will undergo a radical change: all of the water in the tofu, about 86 percent of the total weight, will melt away when thawed, leaving a soft, fine-textured, fine-grained, spongy product especially suited for mixing with meats or using as a meat substitute.

It will take approximately 12 hours to freeze the tofu. Drain it first; then place it in a plastic bag. Frozen tofu may turn a pale yellow or brown color.

A wonderful way to prepare frozen and thawed tofu is batter-dipped. Sliced into 1/2-inch slices, dipped into batter and fried, it can be served alone or on a sandwich with melted cheese on top. Cut into smaller pieces, perhaps 1/2-inch cubes, and batter-fried, it becomes an appetizer — superb when dipped in a seafood cocktail sauce with plenty of horseradish.

BATTER-DIPPED TOFU

1 pound tofu, frozen, thawed, and drained
1 cup unbleached flour
1/2 teaspoon salt
1/8 teaspoon pepper
1 teaspoon dried dill weed
1 egg
1/4 cup milk
3 dashes hot sauce
oil for frying

Cut the tofu into 1/2-inch cubes or slices. Combine the flour with the seasonings. In a separate bowl, beat the egg, and add the milk and hot sauce. Heat the oil in a heavy skillet. Dip the tofu in the flour, then in the egg mixture, and again in the flour. Fry until browned, about 3 minutes on each side.

Yield: 8 to 10 slices
Time: 20 minutes

Making Tofu

Before you embark on this fearsome-looking task, you might ask yourself, Is it really worth it when I can buy tofu at the store? Well, you already know the answer. Is bread better from the oven or from the store? And less expensive too? Homemade is better! And very easy, really.

Once the soybeans have soaked overnight, making tofu will take only about an hour and a half, including cleanup time. It will take even less time as you become experienced.

Equipment

Every gourmet food has its fancy, high-priced equipment to go with its preparation. Tofu is no exception. But if grandmother had made tofu, she would have made it with the kitchen utensils she had on hand, which is what we recommend doing.

We mold our tofu in a colander or several plastic containers perforated with 1/4-inch holes. But, if you want your tofu molded into a perfect rectangle, you can use a cheese form or a tofu press. A tofu press is usually available at kitchen specialty stores or health food stores. The kit includes the wooden tofu box, a pressing sack, cheesecloth, nigari solidifer, and an instruction booklet.

Here is a list of equipment you will need.

- 4-quart (or larger) heat-proof bowl or pan
- blender
- 8-quart (or larger) stainless steel or enamel kettle with lid
- colander
- cheesecloth
- large wooden spoon
- stainless steel or enamel ladle
- measuring cups and spoons
- tofu press or cheese form (optional)

Ingredients

Basically, tofu is coagulated soy milk. Many different coagulants, or solidifiers, are used to make tofu. Each produces a different tasting tofu, but the differences are subtle; choose whatever solidifier is convenient for you.

For 1 pound of soybeans, use 1 of the following solidifiers.

- 3 tablespoons lemon juice, fresh (strained) or frozen
- 3 tablespoons cider vinegar
- 2 teaspoons Epsom salts
- 1-1/2 teaspoons nigari (bittern)

The amounts I have given are approximate. Sometimes you will get a softer or firmer tofu depending on the type or age of bean. With experience, you will learn which solidifier you like and how much of it works best for you.

TOFU-MAKING NOTES

- If your stove burner won't maintain a low heat and your tofu sticks to the pan, try greasing or spraying the pan first with a vegetable oil, or use an asbestos mat over the burner.
- Some people use the bean mash (the pulp left when the soy milk has been extracted, which is called *okara*) in meat loaves, patties, chilies, or in baked goods to contribute fiber. Depending on the age of the soybean, this ingredient is sometimes very coarse. It is high in carbohydrates and does have some nutritional value. Since most of the quality and nutrition of the soybean has gone into making the tofu, you will have to decide for yourself whether the bean mash is worth your while in cooking.
- Whey can be used as a mild soap for dishwashing. Some people use it for soup stocks, and it does have nutritional value; but here again, you are on your own.
- Soy milk can be used in most recipes calling for cow's milk. In cooking, the tastes are satisfactorily similar.
- Tofu, soy milk, whey, and bean mash can be served to your pets for added nutrition. Simply mix it into their regular meal.

Making Tofu
1. Combine 1 cup of soaked soybeans with 1-1/2 cups of water in the blender. Blend until smooth. Repeat until all the beans are blended.

2. Pour the blended beans and water into a large kettle. Bring the contents of the kettle to a boil, then simmer for 20 minutes, stirring frequently.

TOFU RECIPE

1 pound soybeans (2+ cups)
solidifier

Rinse the beans and pick out any bad ones you find. Place the beans in a glass or steel bowl (not aluminum) and cover the beans with water. Let the beans soak overnight. (If anything interferes with your plans to make tofu at this point, you can put the beans in the refrigerator until the next day.)

Drain and rinse the beans again.

Add 2 cups of water to a large stainless steel or enamel kettle, and set the kettle over medium heat.

Combine 1 cup of beans with 1-1/2 cups of water in the blender. Blend until the mix turns milky white, smooth, and foamy — about 40 seconds. Add the blended beans to the kettle and do another cup of beans in the same fashion. Once you have blended all the beans, rinse out the blender with 1 cup of water and add that to the kettle. You will use a lot of water for this step, maybe 15 cups.

Bring the contents of the kettle to a boil; then reduce the heat to simmer, at the lowest heat you have. Cook this mix over low heat for 20 minutes, stirring frequently with a large wooden spoon. More foam may form on the top, and that is fine, just stir it in.

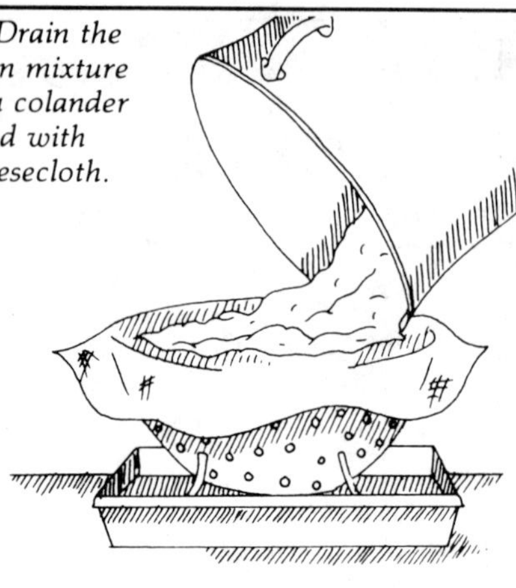

3. *Drain the bean mixture in a colander lined with cheesecloth.*

4. *Squeeze out any excess soy milk. This soy milk will be processed into tofu.*

While the beans are cooking, place a heat-proof container in the sink, large enough to hold all the contents of your kettle. A large roasting pan works well. Put your colander into this container, and line it with several thicknesses of cheesecloth, leaving enough cloth overhanging so that later you can gather it up to squeeze the beans.

Pour the bean mix into the colander. Milky white liquid, "soy milk," will drain into your large bowl or pan. *From this liquid comes the tofu.* Clear the sink for a minute so you can wash and dry the kettle. Pour the soy milk into the cleaned kettle.

Now pour 3 quarts of cold water through the remaining bean mixture, sifting the mashed beans lightly with your hand so that you drain away all possible soy milk. Do not let any beans spill into the soy milk.

Gather the cheesecloth together and squeeze out any remaining milk. Add this soymilk to the kettle.

Bring the contents of the kettle, the soy milk, to a boil, then remove the kettle from the heat. Save or discard the bean mash, then rinse the cheesecloth for a later step.

Put your solidifier into a measuring cup and then add enough water to make 1 cup of liquid and stir well. Pour half of this mixture into the boiled soy milk and stir thoroughly.

Cover the kettle and wait 2 to 3 minutes. Now take a look. Tiny bits of tofu should be floating in a clear yellowish water. Add the rest of the solidifier mix and stir well but gently. Cover the kettle and wait another 3 minutes.

5. Boil the soy milk in a large kettle. Remove from heat and add the solidifier.

6. Strain the soy curds in a colander lined with cheesecloth. Fold the ends of the cheesecloth over the curds, and weight the bundle with something heavy, such as a 1-pound can.

Take another look inside the kettle. What you are after is soft white curds floating in a yellowish liquid. If the liquid is still milky white, make a little more solidifier-water mixture and mix that into the soy milk. Be careful to add solidifier in small amounts; too much makes for a too-firm tofu.

Put the colander back into the sink, lining it again with cheesecloth. Or, line the cheese form, placing it in the colander for stability. Or, line the tofu press with cheesecloth and place it in the sink.

Using a stainless steel or enamel ladle, ladle the whey, or clear liquid, into the waiting mold. Try to strain all the whey you can before putting in the white tofu curds. As you get to the bottom of the kettle, the curds will start to form one big white mass. Finally, gently ladle these curds into the mold.

Fold the ends of the cheesecloth over the top of the curds, place a saucer or something flat on the curds and weight it down with a 1-pound can. Let the tofu drain for at least a half hour. (The longer the pressing time, the firmer the tofu.) This is the time to wash your kettle with cool water. If you wait, the tofu may stick to the pan.

After a half hour, remove the can and saucer. Turn the mold over and remove the cloth-covered tofu. It will be a little more fragile than molded gelatin. Gently peel back the cloth to reveal the results of your work: 1-1/2 pounds of delicate, delicious, homemade tofu.

If you are not going to devour your fresh tofu on the spot with a little soy sauce, place it gently into a bowl or bread pan and cover it with water. It will keep at least a week in the refrigerator, especially if you change the water every other day.

Congratulations! It wasn't that hard, was it? And the taste is better than you expected, isn't it?

One final note: wash and iron your cheesecloth for the next batch of tofu.

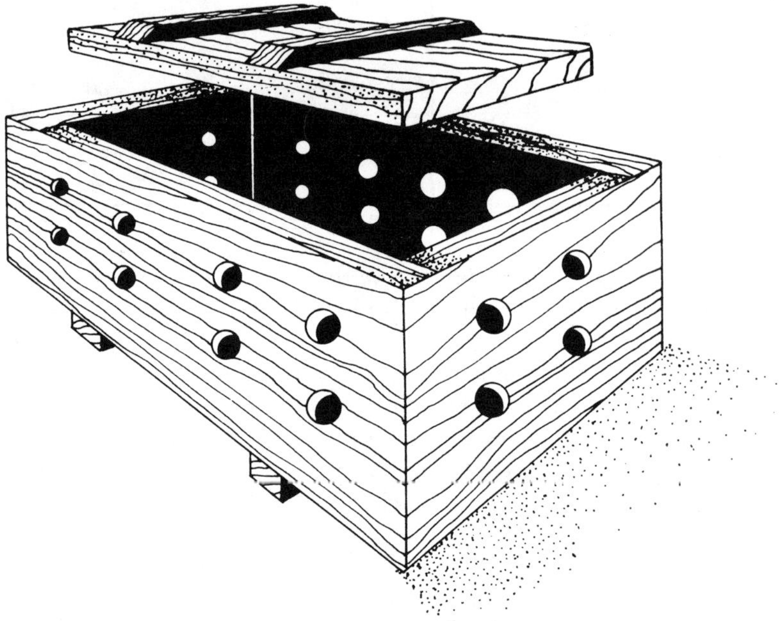

Make your own tofu press with scrap lumber. Holes, 1/2 inch in diameter, are drilled on the sides and bottoms. The top fits inside *the box and can be weighted down to exert extra pressure on the tofu to make a firmer product.*

Tofu on the Side

If tofu is new to you, you might want to try it as a side dish or on salad first. Eventually, you will be serving tofu as the main ingredient in many of your favorite dishes.

SWEET POTATO PANCAKE

An unusual side dish, appetizing in color.

1 cup cooked sweet potato, mashed
4 ounces tofu
2/3 cup fresh bread crumbs
1 tablespoon onion, minced
a few dashes of curry powder
1/4 teaspoon salt
2 tablespoons unbleached flour, spread on a saucer
2 tablespoons oil

Using a fork, mix all the ingredients, except the flour and oil, in a small bowl. Mash the tofu as you mix and blend. Form the mix into 4 thin patties, and dip each side in the flour.

Heat the oil in a heavy skillet, and fry the pancakes over medium-low heat for about 10 minutes on each side. The pancakes should be golden brown and crusty on the outside, soft and rich inside.

Yield: 4 pancakes
Time: 25 minutes

EGG-FREE MAYONNAISE

No mayonnaise? No eggs? On a diet? Tofu mayonnaise has a light and similar taste, although the texture is not as smooth as real mayonnaise.

3/4 cup oil
2 tablespoons lemon juice
1/4 teaspoon prepared mustard
1/4 to 1/2 teaspoon salt
8 ounces tofu

Put all of the ingredients into the blender in the order given. Process until smooth, using a rubber spatula to scrape the sides of the glass. The oil separates again during storage, so stir before using.

Yield: 1-1/4 cups
Time: 5 minutes

OLIVE NUT SPREAD

This spread is good on crackers and even better broiled on a slice of bread. For the best flavor, make this spread in advance and refrigerate it overnight.

1/2 pound tofu, crumbled
10 pitted olives, green *or* **black**
1/3 cup pecan *or* **walnut halves**
1-1/2 ounces cream cheese
dash Worcestershire sauce
1 small garlic clove, minced
a few tablespoons of olive juice, dill pickle juice, *or* **beer**

Place all the ingredients in a blender and process until smooth. Use a spatula to scrape down the sides of the blender to assist the process. Add more juice or beer, a little at a time, to achieve a moist, easily spread consistency. Refrigerate for at least an hour to combine flavors.

Yield: approximately 1-1/4 cups
Time: 10 minutes plus chilling time

POPPY SEED DRESSING

This dressing is great on a spinach-mushroom salad, topped with fresh orange slices or mandarin orange segments from a can. Use less honey if you do not like sweet dressings.

1/4 cup oil
1/4 cup cider vinegar
2 tablespoons lemon juice
1/4 cup honey
6 ounces tofu
1 tablespoon poppy seeds

Place all the ingredients in your blender in the order given. Blend until smooth.

Yield: 1-1/4 cups
Time: about 5 minutes

MARINATED SALAD

1/4 cup vegetable oil
2 tablespoons cider vinegar
1 teaspoon honey
1 teaspoon soy sauce
1 teaspoon dry oregano
1/4 teaspoon garlic salt
a few grinds of black pepper
1 small onion, sliced thinly
1 pound carrots, sliced into 1/4-inch rounds
1 pound green beans, sliced in 1-inch lengths
12 ounces tofu

Pour the oil, vinegar, honey, soy sauce, and seasonings into a large mixing bowl. Add the vegetables and tofu, and toss lightly but thoroughly. Place in a refrigerator container with a tightly fitting lid, and chill several hours, shaking gently or turning upside down occasionally.

Yield: 6 servings
Time: 30 to 35 minutes, plus chilling time

TOMATO TOFU SALAD

This is a very light, protein-packed summer salad.

1/4 cup vegetable oil (olive oil is best)
1/4 cup lemon juice
1/8 teaspoon salt
1/8 teaspoon pepper
1/2 teaspoon dried basil
4 scallions, chopped
1 cup sliced mushrooms
2 medium tomatoes, chopped
8 ounces tofu, cut in 1/2-inch cubes

Combine the oil, lemon juice, and seasonings. Add the vegetables and tofu. Toss gently. Chill for a half hour before serving.

Yield: 4 to 6 servings
Time: 45 minutes

GREEN ONION DIP

Use fresh garlic and green onions in this dip for best flavor.

8 ounces sour cream
8 ounces tofu
1 garlic clove
3 green onions, chopped
1 teaspoon Worcestershire sauce *or* **soy sauce**
salt to taste

In the order given, put all of the ingredients into your blender or food processor, and process until smooth. Serve with chips or fresh vegetables — or pile into hot baked potatoes.

Other dips can be made using various herbs, vegetables, or cheeses to season the tofu and sour cream — just combine your own experience and creativity.

Yield: approximately 2 cups
Time: 3 to 5 minutes

Soups

Tofu is great in soups. It can be used as a thickener in creamy soups or left to float alone in broths or rich vegetable soups. Here are two of my favorite recipes. You will find more soups on pages 27 and 29. Don't be afraid to improvise with tofu in your favorite recipes. You may be surprised at the results — and it is such a good nutritional boost.

CREAM OF MUSHROOM SOUP

Using the bones and scraps from a frying chicken, plus an onion, a stalk of celery, and a carrot, you can boil up at least enough stock for this recipe. Substitute an envelope of vegetable bouillon for the chicken scraps to make a vegetable stock.

2 cups chicken *or* **vegetable stock**
1 cup chopped mushrooms
1 small onion, quartered
1/3 cup brown rice
dash garlic salt
4 ounces tofu
1/2 cup milk
salt to taste

Place the stock, mushrooms, onion, rice, and garlic salt in a saucepan. Bring to a boil; then simmer, covered, until the rice is thoroughly cooked. This will take 30 to 50 minutes. Pour this soup into your blender, and add the tofu and milk. Blend 1 minute, until smooth but still hearty. Salt to taste. Serve immediately, or rewarm slightly if necessary.

Yield: about 3 cups
Time: 50 to 55 minutes

HEARTY VEGETABLE SOUP

1 quart water
3 tablespoons soy sauce
2 teaspoons parsley
1 carrot, chopped
1 potato, diced
2 tomatoes, chopped
1 cup cabbage, chopped
1 cup corn
1 cup summer squash *or* **cucumber, diced**
1 cup peas *or* **pea pods**
8 ounces tofu, cut in bite-size pieces
2 cups spinach *or* **Swiss chard leaves**
salt to taste

Place all the ingredients, except the spinach and salt, in a soup pot and stir well. Bring the soup to a boil, then simmer for 30 minutes. Add the spinach for the last 5 minutes of cooking. This makes a good meal served with corn bread or rye bread fresh out of the oven.

Yield: 4 servings
Time: approximately 1 hour

Thoroughly dry beans can be stored in burlap bags, or loosely covered plastic containers, and kept in a well-ventilated area.

Main Dishes

This is where tofu makes its appearance as a low-calorie, high-protein meat substitute.

TOFU BURGERS

These burgers are good hot or cold — they are great on sesame buns.

1 pound tofu
2 cups rolled oats
1 tablespoon catsup
1 tablespoon Worcestershire sauce
1 small onion, minced
1 teaspoon prepared mustard
1 teaspoon salt
1/4 teaspoon pepper
2 tablespoons butter *or* **safflower oil**
garnishes: lettuce, sliced onions and tomatoes, sprouts, pickles (optional)

Crumble the tofu in a large mixing bowl. Place the oats in your blender and whirl until you have a coarse flour. Add the oats to the tofu, and blend well with a wooden spoon. Add all of the other ingredients, except the garnishes, blending well. Wet your hands and form thin burgers with the mix, making the burgers the size of your bread or bun.

Heat the oil in a heavy skillet. Fry the burgers at a low temperature, about 8 minutes on each side.

Serve on buns or rolls, trimmed with sprouts, lettuce, sliced onions and tomatoes, pickles, or whatever else tickles your fancy.

These burgers freeze well once fried and can be reheated by frying gently in a small amount of oil.

Yield: 6 large burgers
Time: 15 to 20 minutes

QUICHE

Combining cheese, milk, whole wheat, and tofu will give you a perfect combination of proteins — nutritious as well as delicious!

Crust:

- 1 cup whole wheat pastry flour
- dash of salt
- 2 tablespoons butter
- 2 tablespoons oil
- 2 tablespoons ice water

Filling:

- 1/2 pound spinach
- 2 green onions
- 3/4 cup milk
- 2 eggs
- 6 ounces tofu
- 1/4 teaspoon salt
- few grinds of pepper
- dash of nutmeg
- 1/2 cup Swiss *or* Herkimer cheese, shredded

Mix the flour and salt together in a bowl; then add the butter, using a fork to cut it in. Add the oil a little at a time, continuing to cut with the fork until the mixture looks crumbly. Add the ice water and stir until the mixture starts to cling together and can be formed into a ball. Add more ice water if necessary. Flatten the pastry and roll it out between sheets of waxed paper. Spread the crust in an 8-inch pie pan. Poke holes in the crust with a fork. Place in a preheated oven for 5 minutes at 400 degrees F.

Chop the spinach, and wash it by placing it in a dishpan filled with cold water. Swish the chopped spinach around; then let it sit in the water another minute or so to allow the dirt to settle on the bottom. Remove the spinach, and set it aside to drain. Chop the green onions.

Put the drained spinach and chopped onions in a saucepan, covered, over a high heat. The spinach and onions will be soft in about 2 minutes, cooking in the water left on the spinach leaves. Leave the lid off for another minute or so to evaporate *all* of the remaining water.

Then place the vegetables in the waiting pie shell. Put all of the remaining ingredients except the cheese into your blender and process until smooth. Pour this into the pie shell on top of the spinach. Top with cheese and bake at 375 degrees F. for about 50 minutes, or until a clean knife inserted 1 inch from the side of the pan comes out clean. Cool for at least 10 minutes before serving.

Variation: Instead of spinach you can add lean bacon pieces, fried crisp and drained well. Six strips of bacon, broken or cut into bite-size pieces, will suffice. Or you can make a combination quiche of 1/4 pound of wilted spinach and 3 strips of crisp bacon.

Yield: 5 servings
Time: approximately 1-1/2 hours

SPAGHETTI SAUCE

1 medium
1 carrot
1 green pe[illegible]
a handful of mush[illegible] chopped
2 garlic cloves, minced
6 ounces tofu *or* **4 ounces tofu and 4 chicken livers, chopped**
4 tablespoons oil
1 large can tomatoes (1 pound, 12 ounces)
1/2 can tomato paste (3 ounces)
1/2 cup red wine *or* **water**
1 tablespoon parsley
1 tablespoon basil
1 tablespoon oregano
2 bay leaves
salt to taste

Brown the onion, carrot, green pepper, mushrooms, garlic, and tofu (and chicken livers) in the oil for about 3 minutes. Add all of the other ingredients, bring to a boil; then simmer at least 1 hour, loosely covered. Serve over spaghetti.

Yield: approximately 1-1/2 quarts
Time: approximately 1-1/4 hours

TOFU-NUT LOAF WITH MUSHROOM SAUCE

This dish may remind you of meatloaf. It makes a very hearty, informal supper dish. Served cold with horseradish, it tastes amazingly like cold meat.

Tofu Loaf:

1 cup rolled oats
1 cup walnuts
1 pound tofu
1 medium onion, grated
1 carrot, grated
1/2 green pepper, minced
1 teaspoon salt
2 teaspoons sage
2 teaspoons thyme
1 tablespoon oregano

Mushroom Sauce:

3 tablespoons butter
1 shallot *or* 2 scallions, minced
1/2 pound mushrooms, chopped
3 tablespoons unbleached flour
1-1/2 cups milk
dash of garlic salt
a few drops of hot sauce
salt to taste

Preheat your oven to 375 degrees F. Put the oats into your blender and blend until you obtain a coarse flour, stirring with rubber spatula between blendings if necessary. Transfer the oat flour to a large mixing bowl. Put the walnuts into the blender and blend coarsely; then add the nuts to the oats in the bowl.

Crumble the tofu into the bowl and add all of the other ingredients (the vegetables should total 1 cup). Mix well, even beat some, until all ingredients are blended, and the contents of the bowl has a fluffy, but firm, texture. Butter a large shallow casserole dish then add the contents of the bowl, shaping into an oval or a rectangle in the center of the dish. The loaf should be no more than 2 inches high. Bake at 375 degrees F. for 45 minutes, adding half the mushroom sauce during the last 10 minutes of cooking.

To make the mushroom sauce, melt the butter in a skillet, then add the shallot and the mushrooms. Sauté until slightly cooked. Add the flour and blend well. Add all of the other ingredients and bring to a boil, stirring frequently. Turn off the heat. Pour half the sauce over the Tofu-Nut Loaf during the last minutes of cooking time, and serve the rest as gravy.

Yield: about 6 servings
Time: about 1 hour

LASAGNA

3 quarts water
12 lasagna noodles, preferably whole wheat
1 teaspoon salt
1 teaspoon oil
1 small eggplant (3 cups), diced
2 cups carrots, chopped *or* **grated**
2 cups zucchini, chopped
1 cup onion, chopped
2 garlic cloves, minced
5 tablespoons olive oil
1 tablespoon oregano
1 tablespoon basil
2 teaspoons salt
1 large can tomatoes (3-1/2 cups)
1/2 can tomato paste (3 ounces)
1/2 cup sweet red wine
1/2 pound spinach
1/2 cup water
1 pound tofu
2/3 cup Parmesan cheese, grated
1 teaspoon salt
1 cup mozzarella cheese (optional)

Put 3 quarts of water on to boil for the noodles, adding about one teaspoon each of salt and oil.

In a skillet, sauté the eggplant, carrot, zucchini, onion, and garlic in the olive oil for about 3 minutes. Add the oregano, basil, and salt; continue sautéing, stirring frequently, and adding a little more oil if necessary, for 3 more minutes. Then add the tomatoes, tomato paste, and wine; stir well. Cover and simmer for a half hour, stirring frequently.

Meanwhile, boil the noodles for ten minutes and drain into a colander.

Chop and cook the spinach in a little water over high heat. Drain.

Place a half cup of water and tofu into your blender, then blend, adding the cooked spinach. Spoon into a bowl, then beat in the Parmesan cheese and salt.

To assemble the lasagna, spoon a thin coating of the vegetable sauce into the bottom of a 13-inch by 9-inch pan or casserole dish. Make 1 layer of noodles, using 4 strips. Spoon 1/3 of the tofu mixture here and there on the noodles, covering each mound with a spoonful of sauce, for ease in spreading. Spread the filling over the noodles with the back of a spoon. Repeat the noodle-tofu-sauce layers three times. Top with grated mozzarella cheese if desired.

Bake at 325 degrees F. for 45 minutes; then let the lasagna sit for 15 minutes, out of the oven, if you can wait that long. The lasagna will firm up as it cools, and the flavors will blend into perfection.

Yield: 6 servings
Time: approximately 2 hours

GRILLED CHEESE-TOFU SANDWICH

Slice tofu thinly and place enough on one slice of bread to cover it all the way to the edges. Top with thinly sliced cheddar cheese. For a little excitement, add sliced pickles, sliced onions, or a few dashes of hot sauce. Put another slice of bread on top and butter both slices (outsides) for grilling; or dip the sandwich into a mixture of beaten egg and milk and fry as you would French toast.

CURRIED VEGETABLES

Creamy cubes of tofu contrast nicely with the texture of the bite-size vegetables. This is a vegetable toss taken out of the ordinary.

4 tablespoons oil
1 clove of garlic, minced
a few dashes of curry powder (more to taste)
6 ounces tofu, cubed
1 bunch broccoli, chopped
2 large carrots, sliced thinly on the diagonal
1 onion, sliced thinly
2 tomatoes, chopped
salt to taste

Heat the oil in a large skillet or wok. When the oil is hot, but not smoky, add the minced garlic. Sauté for a minute. Remove the garlic, and add a few dashes of curry powder and the tofu cubes. Sauté the cubes, stirring frequently, for about 3 minutes.

Add the vegetables one at a time. First add the broccoli and sauté for about 2 minutes; then add the carrots and onion. Continue stirring and tossing over low heat. When the carrots are tender and the onions appear translucent — after 3 minutes or so — add the tomatoes to heat through, about 2 more minutes. Salt to taste.

This makes a great meal served with rice. Try a little yogurt on the side.

Yield: 5 to 6 servings
Time: 20 to 30 minutes

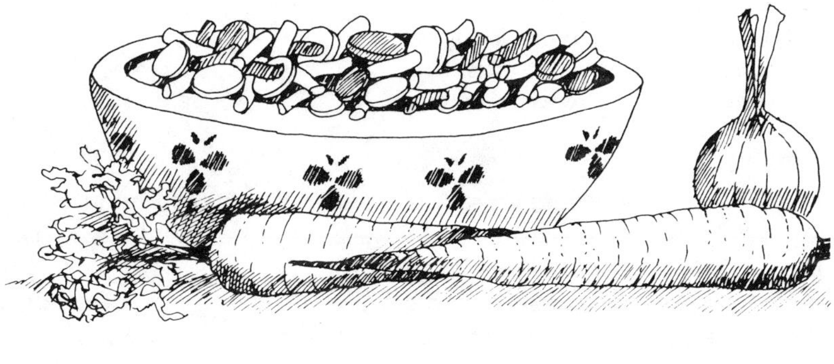

Chinese Dishes

In Chinese cooking, the bland flavor of tofu is often used to complement other strongly flavored ingredients. Some of the ingredients may be new to you; but if you are lucky enough to live near an oriental food store, you will find every ingredient we mention. Be sure to check the gourmet food section of your supermarket, too; they may carry these special items.

If you are not used to spicy foods, these dishes may taste a little strong to you, so experiment with quantities.

EGGPLANT SZECHUAN STYLE

This recipe calls for sesame oil, which adds a smoky taste, and hot sesame oil, which is very hot, and vegetable oil. Vary the proportions of oils to achieve different tastes. The recipe offered here is quite mild.

1 small eggplant (1/2 to 3/4 pound)
1 teaspoon salt
1 tablespoon hot sesame oil
1 tablespoon sesame oil
1 tablespoon vegetable oil
1/2 teaspoon salt
1/4 cup soy sauce
3/4 pound fresh *or* **frozen string beans**
8 ounces tofu, cut in 1/4-inch cubes
2 tablespoons sesame seeds (optional)

Peel the eggplant, and cut it into 1/4-inch cubes. Sprinkle the eggplant with 1 teaspoon of salt, and allow it to sit for 5 minutes or more. The salt will draw out the bitterness in the eggplant. Rinse the salt off before cooking the eggplant.

Heat the oils in a wok or large skillet. Add 1/2 teaspoon salt, then the eggplant. Fry the eggplant over high heat for 5 minutes or until the eggplant becomes quite soft. (If the oil starts to smoke, reduce the heat.) Add the soy sauce and continue stirring for another minute. Add the string beans and tofu, and continue cooking until the string beans are tender but not soft. Toss in the sesame seeds and serve immediately with plenty of hot rice.

Yield: 4 servings
Time: 25 minutes

BEAN CURD SOUP

1 quart homemade chicken stock, clarified if desired
1/4 cup finely minced green onions (reserve some tops)
2 tablespoons dried green seaweed *or* **finely chopped spinach**
8 ounces tofu, cut in 1/2-inch cubes
4 tablespoons celery leaves, chopped fine
soy sauce

The appearance of this soup is greatly enhanced if you use clarified soup stock. To clarify stock, start with only fresh meat, bones, and vegetables. After simmering the stock at least 1 hour, let the stock boil down, uncovered, until you have a good strong flavor. Strain the stock through a cheesecloth. Briefly place a piece of paper towel on top of the soup to remove any surface grease. Place the stock in a clean soup pot with one egg white and one broken egg shell. Bring to a boil and let simmer until the soup is beautiful and clear. Strain through a cheesecloth. You now have clarified your soup stock.

Bring the stock to a boil, then add the green onions and dried seaweed or spinach. Cover the pot, and boil the stock for about 5 minutes; then turn off the heat. Add the tofu cubes and wait a minute or two, until they are heated through. Just before serving, garnish with the green onion tops and celery leaves. Serve in rice bowls with wide spoons, accompanied by a good soy sauce.

Yield: 4 servings
Time: 2 hours

BRAISED TOFU

1 pound tofu, sliced 1/4-inch thick
2 tablespoons vegetable oil
1 clove garlic, sliced thinly
1/2 teaspoon ginger *or* **3 thin slices of fresh ginger root**
3 scallions, chopped
3 tablespoons soy sauce
1/4 cup sauterne

Slice the tofu and spread it out on a flat surface covered with a towel. Weight the tofu with a heavy plate to squeeze out any excess water. Allow the tofu to stand for at least a half hour. Or, use frozen tofu that has been thawed and drained.

Heat the oil in a wok or heavy, 10-inch skillet. Add the garlic and ginger. Gently place the tofu slices in the oil. Fry over medium heat for 2 minutes on each side. Sprinkle the scallions and pour the sauterne and soy sauce on top of the tofu.

Cover. Reduce the heat to low and braise the tofu for 15 minutes. Serve immediately.

Yield: 4 servings as a side dish
Time: 40 minutes

STIR-FRY VEGETABLES

1 tablespoon oil
2 tablespoons soy sauce
2 teaspoons honey
2 garlic cloves, minced
1 tablespoon ginger root, grated
2 cups snow pea pods
2 cups bean sprouts
2 cups bok choy (Chinese cabbage), chopped on a diagonal
1/2 cup green onions, chopped lengthwise
8 ounces tofu, cut in small cubes

Place the oil, soy sauce, honey, and seasonings in a heavy skillet or wok, and heat until sizzling. Spread the mixture around. Add the vegetables and stir fry, gently mixing and tossing over the high heat. Add the tofu. Stir fry until the vegetables begin to look cooked, the tofu is well seasoned, and the bean sprouts have lost their "raw" taste. Serve immediately.

Yield: serves 4 as a side dish, or 2 as a main course, over rice
Time: approximately 15 minutes

HOT AND SOUR SOUP

This is a very special recipe — delicious, aromatic, and authentic.

1 tablespoon salt
1/2 teaspoon honey
2 tablespoons soy sauce
2 tablespoons cider vinegar
1 teaspoon black pepper
1 tablespoon sesame oil
1 fresh scallion, chopped
1 teaspoon ginger, freshly minced
1/4 pound fresh lean pork, cut in matchstick-size pieces (optional)
1 teaspoon soy sauce
1 teaspoon corn starch
5 cups water
1 cup fresh mushrooms, chopped fine
1 pound tofu, chopped fine
1 cup celery *or* **cucumber, chopped fine**
2-1/2 tablespoons corn starch
2 tablespoons cold water
1 egg beaten

In a large bowl combine the first eight ingredients. Set aside. Mix the pork strips with the soy sauce and corn starch.

Bring water to a boil in a large saucepan. Add the pork strips, stirring well. Keep the contents of the pan boiling as you add the mushrooms, tofu, and celery. Boil 3–5 more minutes and thicken with the corn starch combined with water. Stir to a boil, then add the beaten egg.

Remove from heat immediately and pour over the ingredients in the large bowl. Mix gently and serve hot.

Yield: 8 servings
Time: 1 hour

Desserts

Here are some interesting dessert recipes. Developing these recipes proved to be quite a challenge. What we learned is that tofu and chocolate work well together, and so does tofu and mild flavors, such as banana. We hope you will enjoy these recipes, too, and use them as a springboard to develop your own nutritious, low-calorie desserts.

BANANA-APPLE SHAKE

Here's another example of tofu's versatility. You'd never guess this rich shake has no ice cream or milk in it. For best results, chill all the ingredients and the glasses before you begin.

Bananas can be frozen (and used in this shake) by removing their skins and cutting them, if desired; then placing them in a plastic bag. They will keep for at least a month. Our supply has never lasted longer than that.

1/2 cup apple juice *or* **cider**
1/4 cup ripe banana
1/4 cup tofu

In a measuring cup, put 1/2 cup of apple juice. Add enough ripe banana to make 3/4 cup of liquid. Last, add enough tofu to bring the level to the 1-cup line. Dump all ingredients into the blender and blend until very smooth, about 40 seconds. Serve in a chilled glass with a straw.

Yield: 1 shake
Time: 3 minutes

HEAVENLY PIE

This rich pie, or cheesecake, will puff up, then settle and crack like most desserts of its kind. You can cover or decorate the pie with whipped cream after it has cooled, if you so desire.

Crust:

2 cups crushed graham crackers
1/4 cup melted butter
2 tablespoons honey

Filling:

8 ounces cream cheese, softened
8 ounces tofu
1 egg
6 ounces carob *or* **milk chocolate morsels, melted**
1 teaspoon vanilla
whipped cream (optional)

To make the crust combine the cracker crumbs, butter, and honey. Press into an 8-inch pie pan.

In a food processor, or with a mixer at medium speed, blend together the cream cheese, tofu, egg, chocolate, and vanilla. You will find that scraping down the sides of the bowl periodically with a rubber spatula will be neccessary to allow you to blend all the ingredients. Be sure that all the cream cheese lumps are incorporated.

Spoon the chocolate filling into the pie pan. Bake at 350 degrees F. for 30 to 45 minutes. Chill well before serving.

Yield: serves 6 to 8
Time: 1 hour plus chilling time

MILK SHAKE

Tofu adds to the nutritional value of a milk shake and contributes a frothy, light taste.

1 scoop carob *or* chocolate ice cream
1 scoop tofu
1 ounce carob chips, melted *or* 1 tablespoon chocolate syrup
1/2 cup milk

Blend the ingredients together until frothy and smooth.

Yield: 1 shake
Time: 2 minutes

TOFU-PRUNE WHIP

This makes a creamy, rich dessert or breakfast treat. Add honey or sugar to taste, nuts or cereal for crunchiness.

1 cup prunes
1/2 cup juice (from cooked prunes)
8 ounces tofu
2 tablespoons honey
pinch of salt
1/3 cup coarsely chopped pecans *or* walnuts
whipped cream (optional)

Place the prunes in a small pan and cover them with water. Bring them to a boil and then simmer until soft, about 15 minutes. Remove the prunes from the pan and set aside to cool. Boil the prune-water down until you have about 1/2 cup prune juice.

When the prunes are cool enough to handle, pit and chop them. Then put all of the ingredients, except the nuts and whipped cream, into the blender and process, using a rubber spatula to scrape down the sides between blendings. Add the nuts to this mixture, then turn into 4 buttered, 6-ounce custard cups. Bake at 350 degrees F. for about 30 minutes. Serve warm, with whipped cream if desired.

Prune whip can be served cold, too, and without baking. Simply turn the blended mixture into unbuttered dessert dishes and chill.

Yield: 4 to 6 servings
Time: approximately 45 minutes